the Unspoken Life

Coloring Book

Illustrations by Matthew Salaiz

KIMBERLY POPE-ROBINSON, DVM, CCFP

The Unspoken Life Coloring Book

Kimberly Pope-Robinson
1 Life Connected Consulting

Published by 1 Life Connected Consulting
1 Life Connected Consulting
1551 Union Street Unit 205
San Diego, CA 92101

ISBN: 978-0-9986726-3-2

Publishing and editorial team: Author Bridge Media,
www.AuthorBridgeMedia.com
Project Manager and Editorial Director: Helen Chang
Editor: Jenny Shipley
Illustrator: Matthew Salaiz
Design: Najdan Mancic, Iskon Design

Ordering Information:
Quantity sales. Special discounts are available on quantity purchases by corporations, associations, and others. For details, contact the publisher at the address above.

Printed in the United States of America

Dedicated to
Pancho the poop
eater and Sanjay
the Monkey Cat.
Who are both
forever in our
hearts.

Acknowledgements

Kim's husband Jeff, for his unconditional support and always believing in her crazy ideas. Kim's parents and sister for constantly being there, no questions asked for both her and this movement. Of course Isabelle, Graciebird, and Maui, who are big balloon fillers for many. Matt's father for late nights on the big chair together watching David Attenborough documentaries. Matt's mother for recognizing his passion for art at the age of 8, inside of a garage full of oil paintings. To the entire team at Author Bridge who were a critical piece on this coloring book idea becoming a reality, you are an amazing group of individuals and we loved working with you on this project. And finally to the 1 Life Connected community, for encouraging this movement and helping to provide the strength for the persistence to keep moving forward.

Turning into the Culture as We Swim toward Sustainability

I started the 1 Life Connected movement in 2015 with the goal of helping people find their path toward a sustainable career within the veterinary industry so they can connect their careers with their passions.

Walking away from complete financial freedom and starting a movement in a totally foreign, uncharted space was a drastic step, but I was motivated by the belief that if my message saved one person, then it was all worth it. Traveling this path has not been easy, and, at times, I've found myself having to dig deep into living the framework of the message to keep moving forward.

Along this journey, I have often found myself swimming in the "ocean of shame" that I speak of in my book, *The Unspoken Life*. This ocean is the place where sinkers—negative thoughts and feelings—drag me down into a space where I feel unworthy of acceptance and belonging, where I feel my entire worth as a human being is in jeopardy.

Many of us grasp why the veterinary profession can be a sea of sinkers. Whether it's Yelp, Dr. Google, clients with no money, pets with no medical options, malpractice concerns, judgment errors, or all those journals we never read, the sinkers are plentiful.

Even in calmer seas, we in this profession tend to swim in an identical direction, creating our existing industry culture. As sinkers present themselves, we enter into fight-or-flight mode. Our heart rate and blood pressure both rise as we take defensive action. We congregate, looking to use the strength of the group, like a school of fish moving in unison to fight off a threat, and create an atmosphere of "us against them."

Picture this battle-ready school of fish surrounded by what I call the cynical serpent—the "name-blame-judge" monster. To save ourselves, we feed that serpent with judgment, hatred, and blame. This is often directed outward—"clients are stupid, and you can't fix stupid"—but it can also be turned inward—"I'm stupid, and you can't fix me."

As we united to feed the name-blame-judge serpent and deal with our sinkers, I personally found myself becoming more and more disengaged from the world around me. I felt distraught, gradually losing my passion for life, until I felt completely disconnected from humanity.

The current I believed would support me and my fellow vet professionals had abandoned us, so I started swimming in another direction. Although difficult at first, moving away from that name-blame-judge mentality and towards a new one, that of "recognize-embrace-connect," empowered me.

As I began this journey to find a current that supports a culture of my individual desires, wants, and needs, I was excited to see that I wasn't alone in the ocean. Often, I saw other fish attempting to change direction. Sometimes they would be right next to me, and swimming with them made it so much easier to make forward progress, even if our ultimate destinations were different.

To be clear, there is no one "right" direction to follow. There is no one "fix" for the profession, because we are not broken; we are all swimming in that ocean of shame, looking to honor ourselves while we hold up the veterinary oath. For me, that required moving away from feeding the cynical serpent and toward a space where I could hold both my sinkers and my balloons. The balloons are those things that help to lift us out of that ocean of shame and allow us to find ways to stay connected to ourselves and all of humanity. It is not about replacing the sinkers with balloons, but in fact recognizing, embracing, and connecting with both.

We are not broken. We don't need to be fixed. And we are not alone.

This coloring book is intended to allow each of you to take your first steps on a personal journey to career sustainability—to begin swimming against the current of name-blame-judge and move in the direction of recognize-embrace-connect.

Now it's time to find some crayons or a stack of colored pencils. Color along and take your unique fish on the journey back to connection.

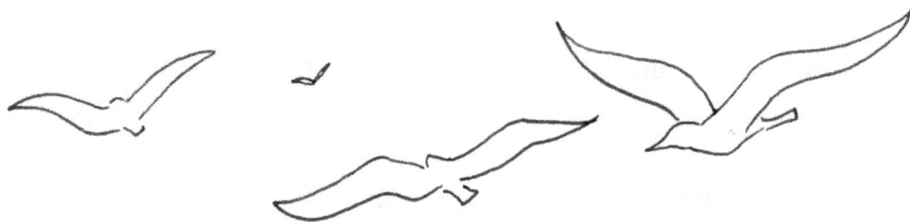

At first we relish the journey
Fighting to save all lives
One day we wake up topsy-turvy
Realizing we've lost our drive

Loneliness and shadows abound
We begin to feel trapped
Smiles fade to frowns
Feeling lost lives untapped

We recognize deep in our core
A life as yet unspoken for

To see where we are
We must first recognize painful emotions
Finding out who we are
Helps us to embrace our devotion

Once we take that first step
We begin to make the correction
One foot forward, then the next
We create our own bridge to connection

We each have our own soul horse
To transport us to love and delight
We work to start on this new course
To reconnect with our own inner light

Sinkers appear all around
While balloons rise above for our reach
Sinkers feed the serpent dragging us down
Balloons lift us up to the beach

Vulnerability gives us discernment:
Our name-blame-judge habit does destroy
In choosing recognize-embrace-connect
A new path reawakens our joy

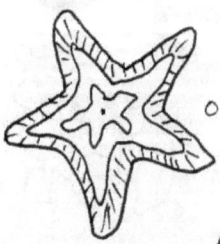

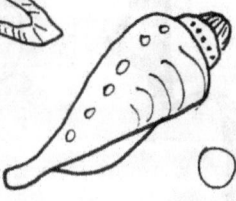

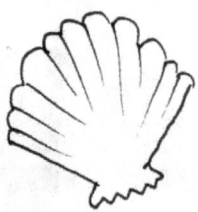

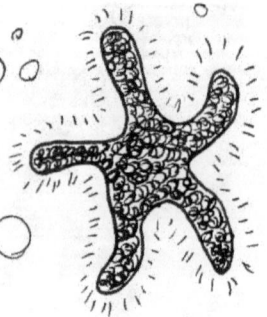

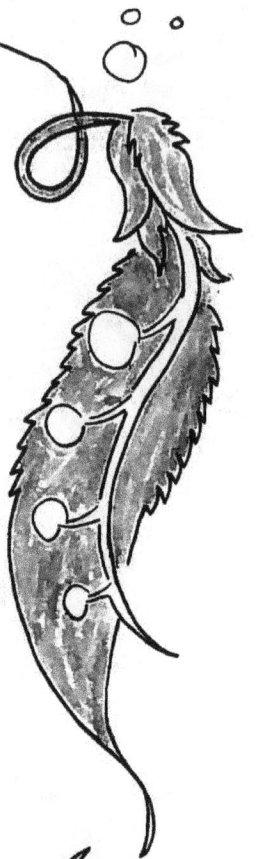

The negativity bias is why we exist today
This doesn't make us bad creatures
We fight to allow ourselves to be okay
Sinkers and balloons our elected features

The principles we seek to understand
Are numbered one through seven
The time to embrace them now at hand
Our lives we seek to leaven

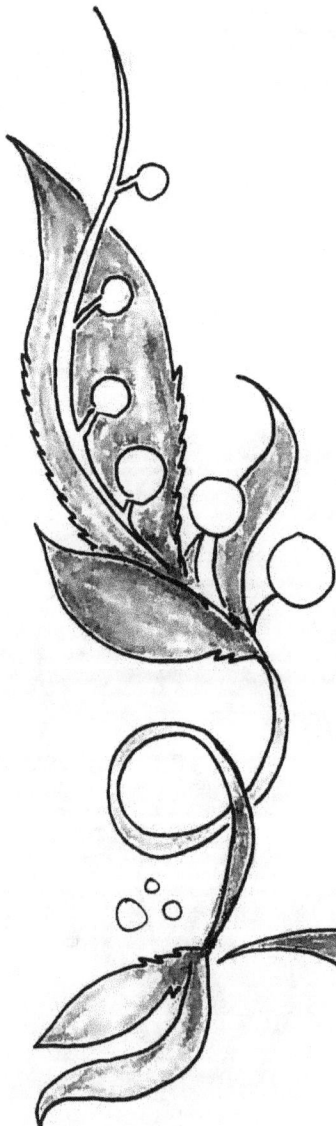

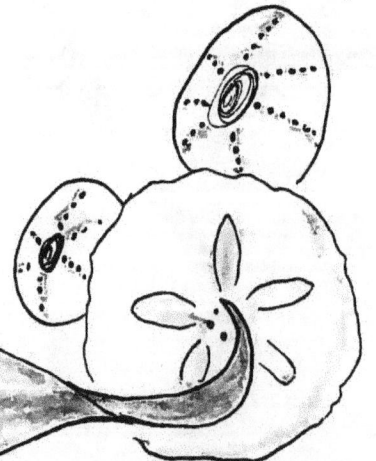

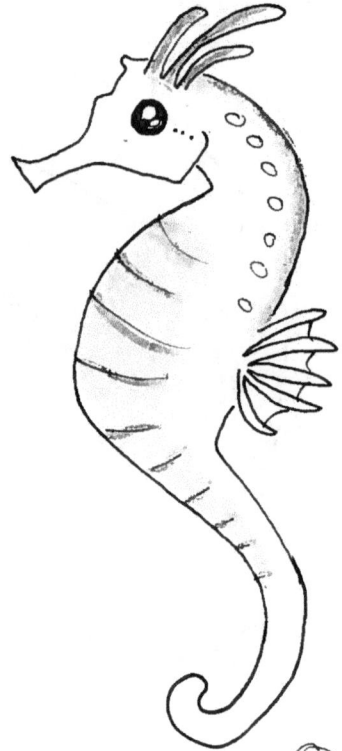

Our uniqueness leads our turnaround
Away from fear and resentment
Even so, we may put others down
Thinking it will lead us to contentment

We judge harshly when others have spoken
This hinders our power to thrive
Then one day we find we've awoken
Truth and self-worth renews our drive

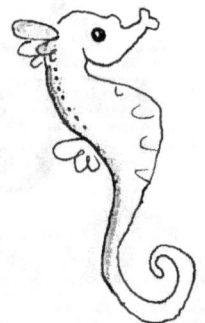

Self-worth begets

True-seeing

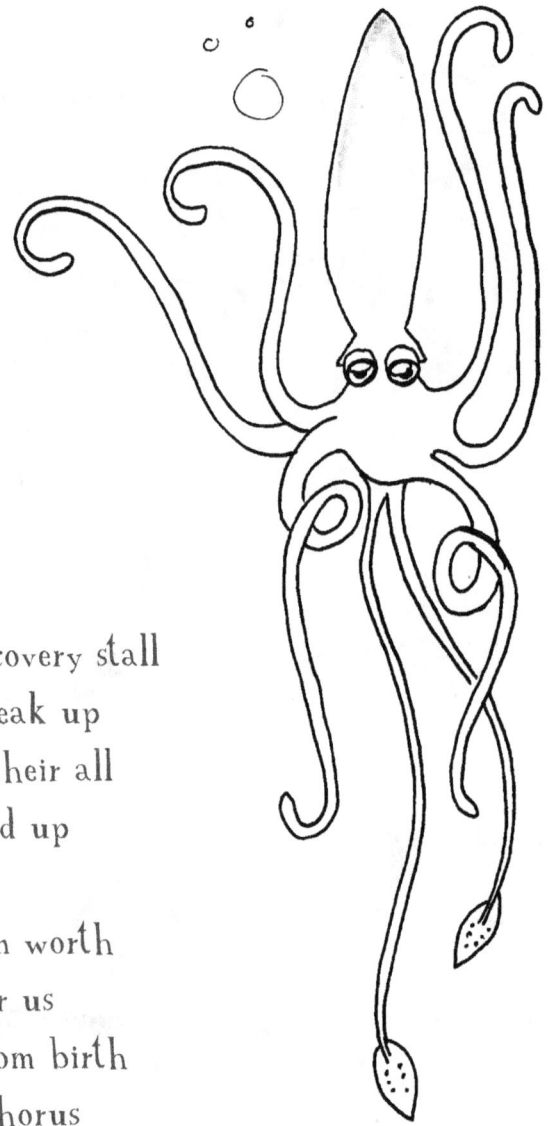

Standing on the edge of the recovery stall
We find we're scared to speak up
Starting to see our lives in their all
We finally begin to stand up

Only we can define our own worth
No other can do this for us
Each of us has substance from birth
Our value embraced in chorus

For our self-worth and uniqueness
Start us on the bridge to completeness

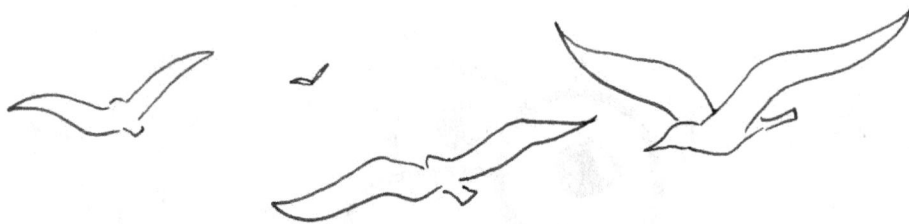

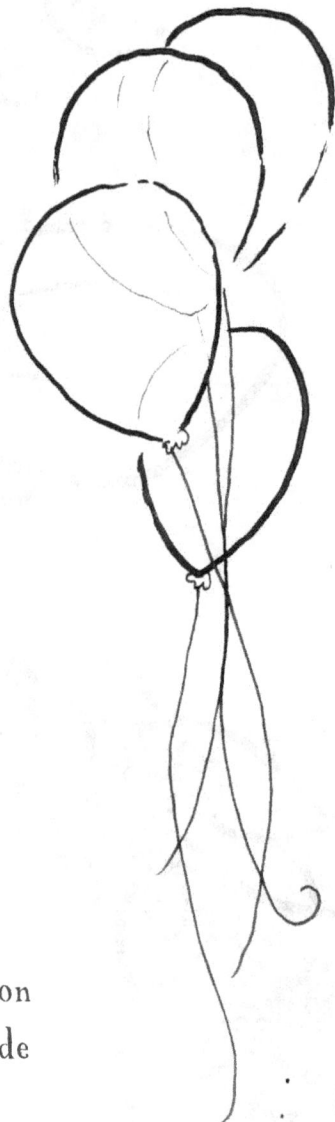

In this journey to honor all creatures
We start out excited for the path to be
But loss and suffering are hard teachers
Soon sacrifice becomes all we see

We fall into our save-the-animal mode
Our passion and sinkers drive this conviction
Each uniquely living out the veterinary code
Bringing us a strong sense of direction

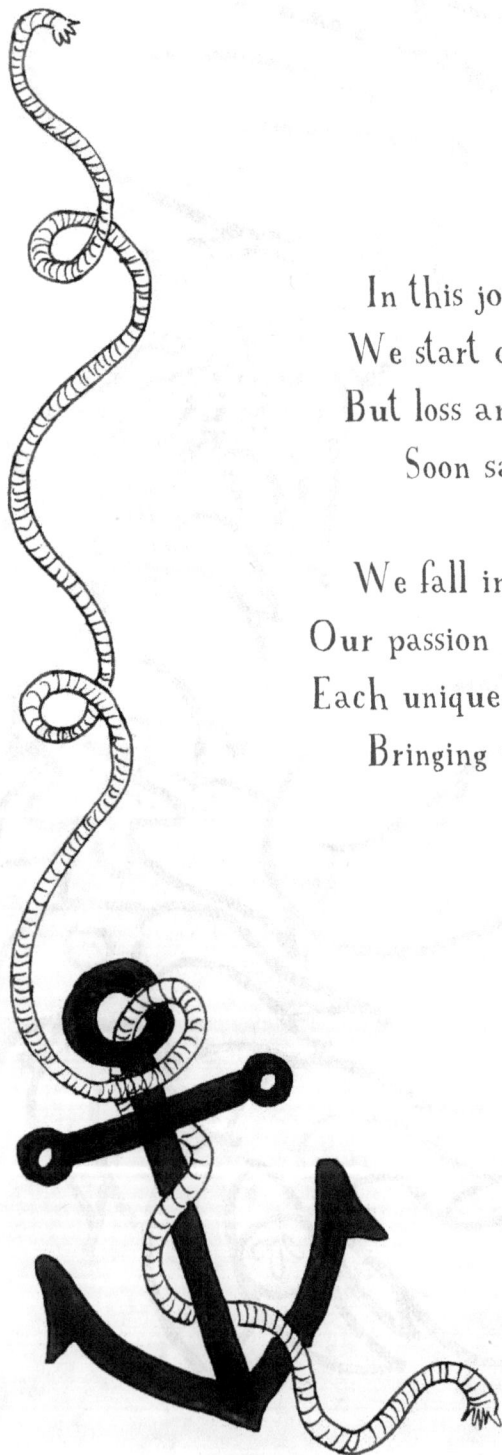

WOOF!

We wake up to see that reality
Is not how we thought we would feel
We fight to find individuality
But the sinkers are all too real

Conviction is that next step in the bridge
It motivates us to keep up our pace
Standing on the edge of the ocean ridge
We begin to create a personal space

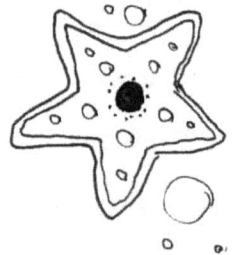

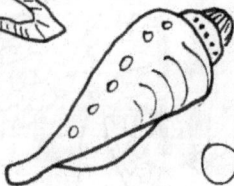

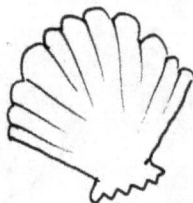

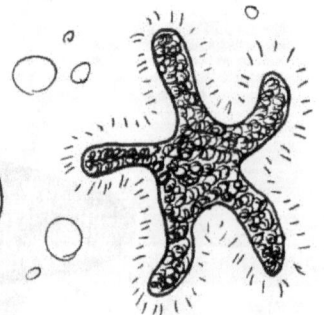

The next step on the bridge is acceptance
Though it is harder to recognize
Only through mistakes and self-forgiveness
Can we see the world through clear eyes

We can accept the unusual on occasion
For those situations do not define who we are
Sinkers often feel like a common recreation
Accepting all parts of our job will take us far

Imperfection is harder to embrace
We all have our own soap cookies
Moments of growth are not meant for retrace
They sure can make us feel like rookies

No situation is meant for us to simply fail
We find our value through interactions we share
Learning and forgiving helps us not to derail
The gift horse each experience brings to bear

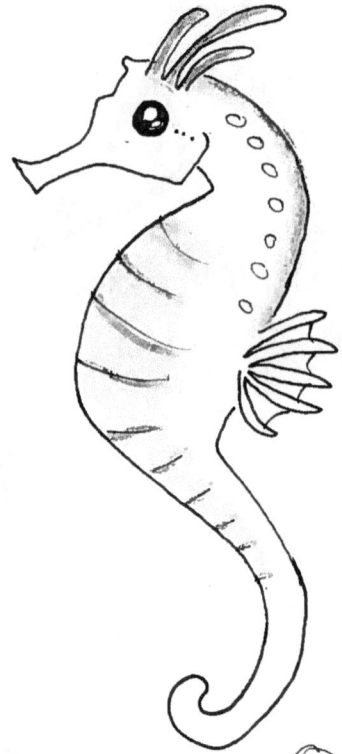

Courage arises in our moving forward
Looking to act, even when against the norm
We find our own "Tough Mudder" to move toward
Though between outcomes we often feel torn

We remember the hurt from the past
Scared to again feel that same pain
Leaving fear behind us at last
It takes courage to find your own lane

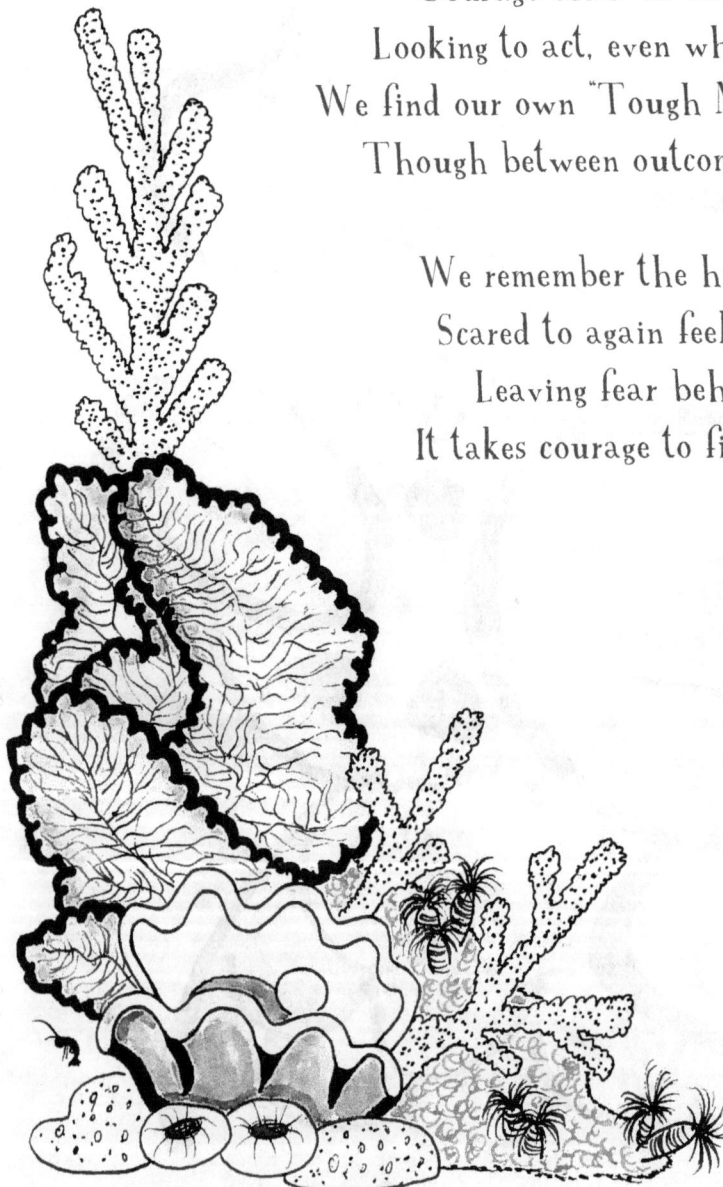

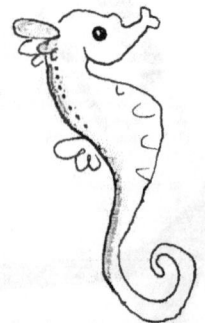

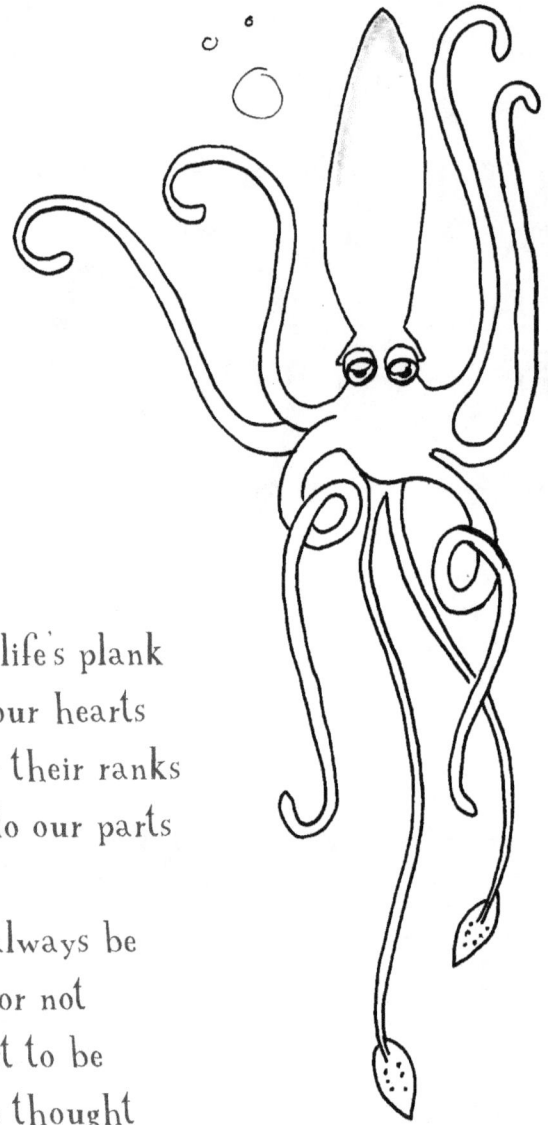

We find ourselves frozen upon life's plank
Fear welling up from risking our hearts
We categorize dangers and order their ranks
Fighting in the process to still do our parts

A risk that is real and will always be
We decide to take action or not
In courage is where we elect to be
And we're not as alone as we thought

Here is where we choose to see
That the solution was always within me

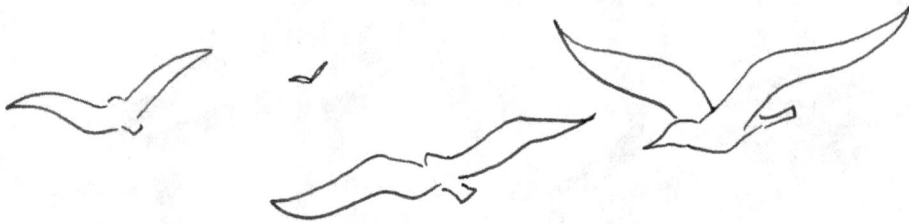

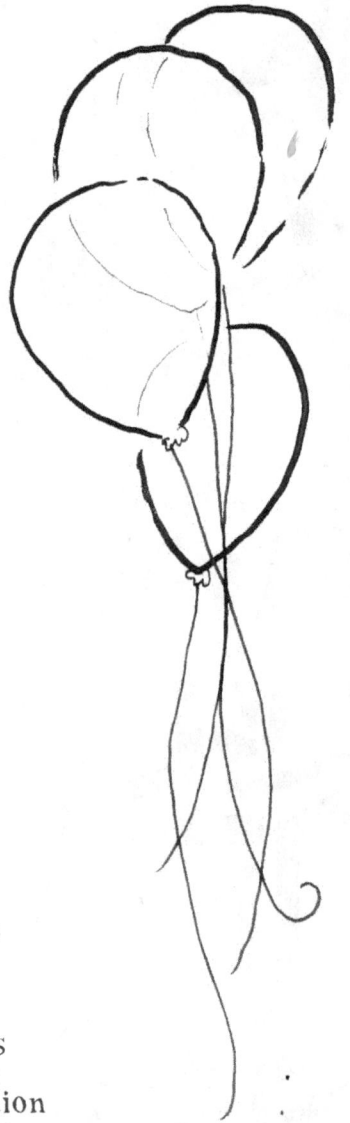

To keep ourselves from sinking
We seek antidotes to shame
To counteract this path of thinking
We find empathy is our aim

We fight our own brown-gauze moments
Our fears spreading infection
We work to find empathy, not opponents
'Til we walk once more the path to connection

Empathy

Caregivers' guilt is ours to own
We must find ourselves neither right nor wrong
The pathway to empathy finally shown
Once we each find our authentic song

Upon society's pedestal we're thrust
A great height from which to fall
The path back down built on empathy and trust
We don't have to agree with it all

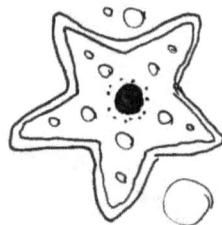

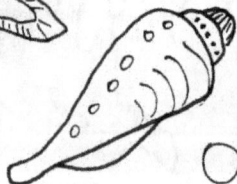

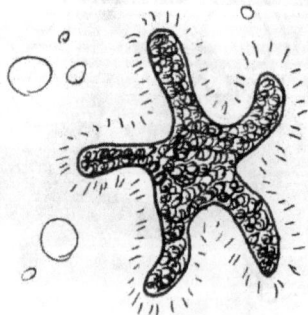

Resilience is what fills our balloons
Helping us to keep moving
It gives us lift when we're running on fumes
Driving us to keep on grooving

We will be pushed toward feeling sad
For the sinkers cannot be stopped
We will be pulled into feeling mad
A sensation as if we were dropped

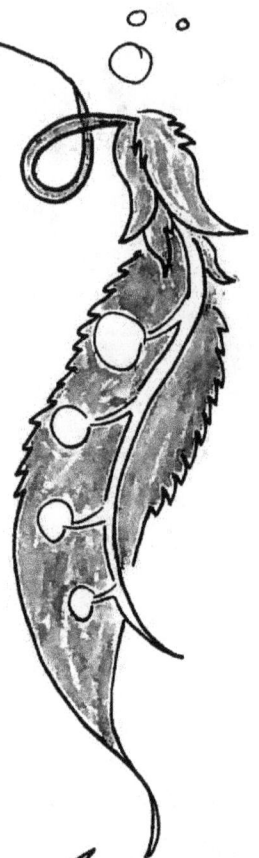

At times we feel anything but good
When we're hurt and weary and worn
We elect not to surrender, although we could
Fighting to get our balloons reborn

Working to stay connected to all
We look for and find our candles
Realizing sinkers are around the bend with each call
We grab our happiness by its handles

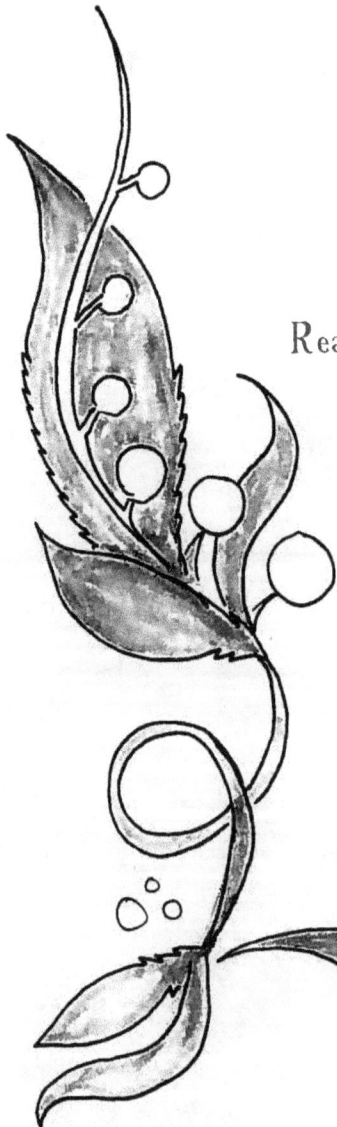

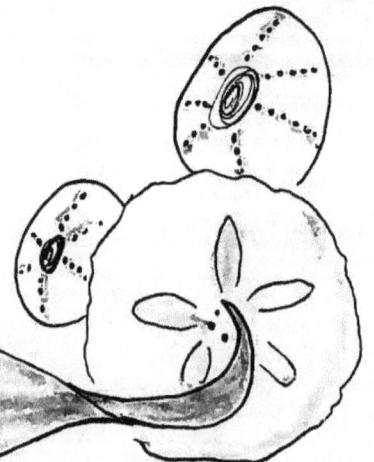

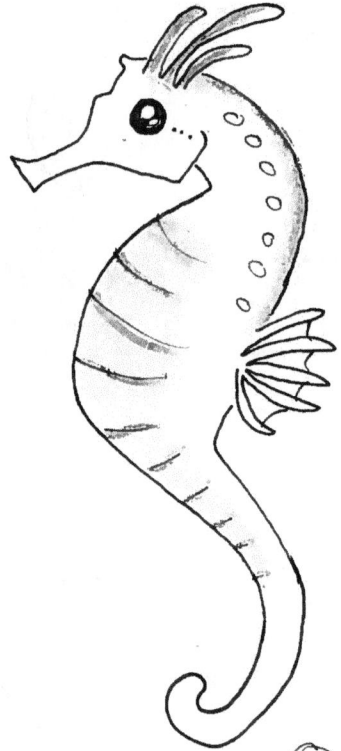

Vision is the final piece
For things are bigger than me
Without vision we have no release
Value starts as I live as "we"

Sharing my journey has changed my life
Looking to help just one person with this story
No longer silenced in the unspoken life
Together, we can all find our glory

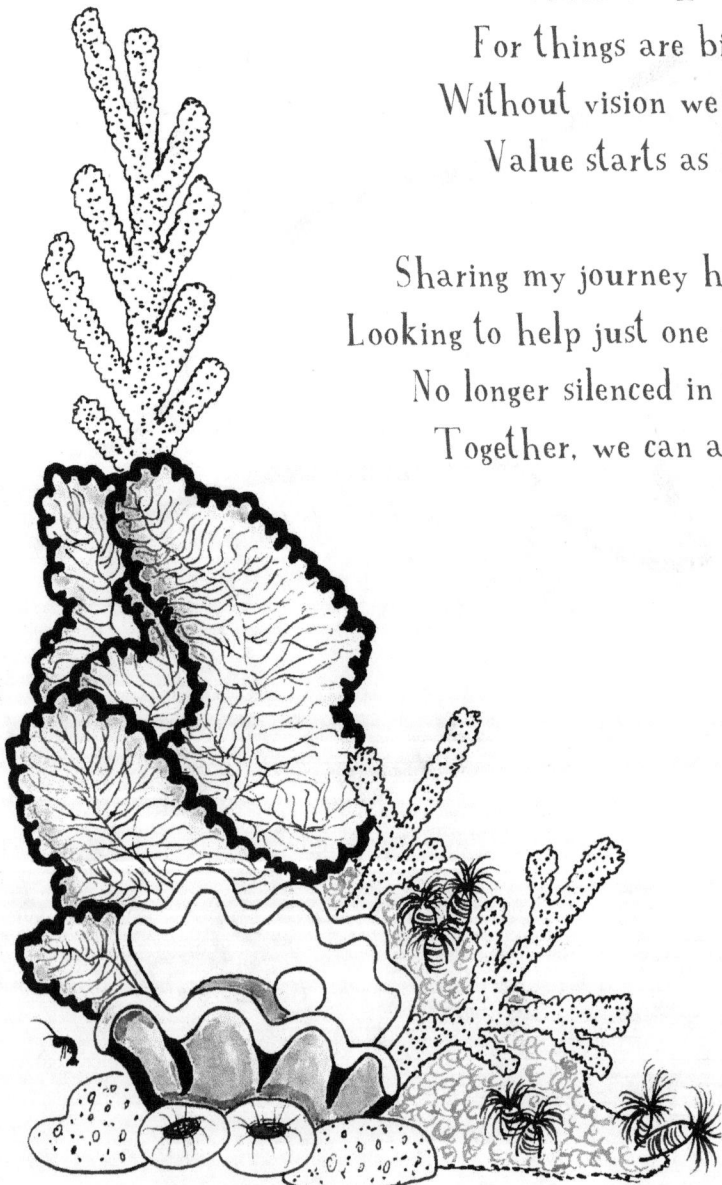

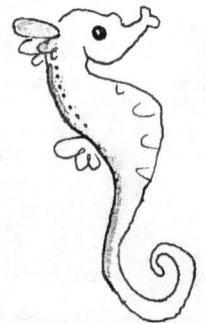

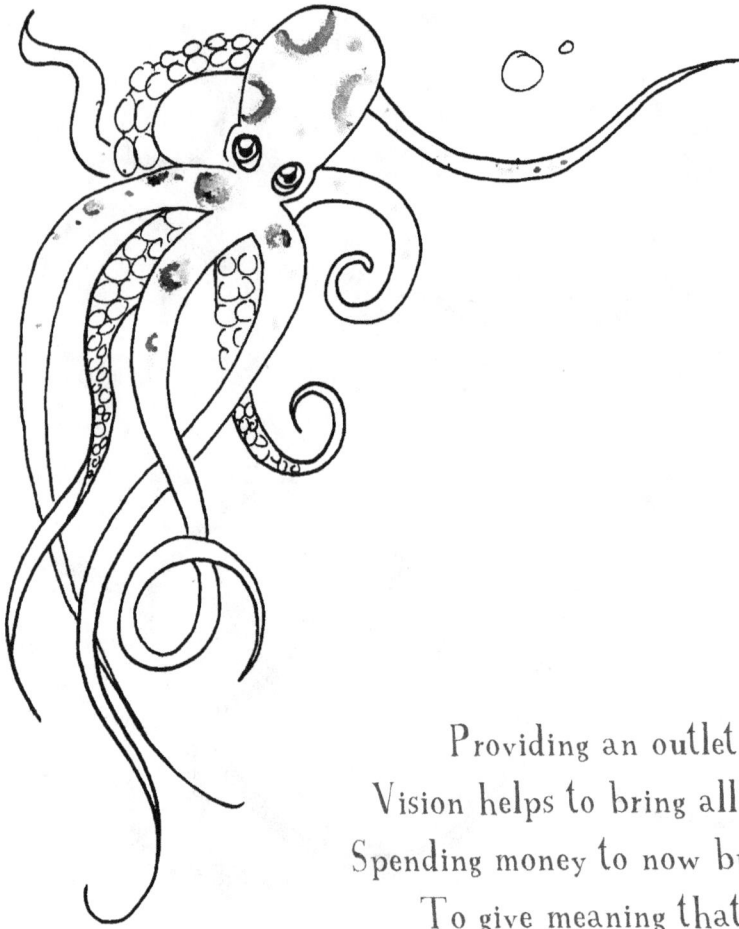

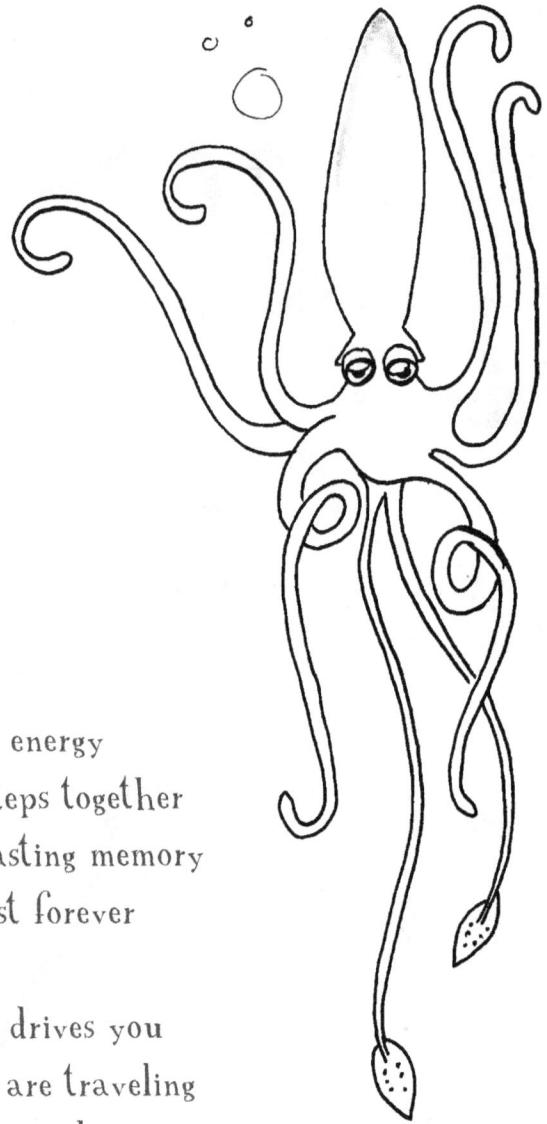

Providing an outlet for our energy
Vision helps to bring all these steps together
Spending money to now build a lasting memory
To give meaning that will last forever

Grounded with the vision that drives you
Now you've chosen the path you are traveling
Your voice no longer unspoken, askew
Your connection no longer at risk of unraveling

1. L . C . C

Now all seven stops have been explored
It is time you begin your walk
For your unique path to be your reward
Staying connected, you must start to talk

Though at times speaking truth feels a chore
Our frame work in hand, we see our choice
And the value of a life that is spoken for
Requires each of us to use our own voice

In the end my life was deserving
Of the fight to see my course corrected
What awaited me, a faith unswerving
Let's all live one life connected

Kimberly Pope-Robinson DVM, CCFP
1 Life Connected

Recognize and Embrace

Connect

About the Author

Dr. Kimberly Pope-Robinson is a sought-after speaker and the founder of 1 Life Connected. She has served in the veterinary field for more than twenty years. After graduating from the UC Davis School of Veterinary Medicine in 2000, she practiced in both the large and the small animal sectors. In 2007, Dr. Pope transitioned into a leadership position for a corporate veterinary practice, and then to a position in the pharmaceutical industry, where she worked with veterinary specialists and colleges of veterinary medicine. During this time, Dr. Pope supported hundreds of veterinarians and their teams.

Dr. Pope's career experience provided her with a unique exposure to the stresses of the veterinary profession. This gave her a strong understanding of the lack of fulfillment often found in the profession. Since then, Dr. Pope has worked to help others manage their perfectionist tendencies, confront their personal shame, and develop the skills of self-forgiveness and resilience. These became cornerstones of 1 Life Connected, through which veterinarians build the foundation for a sustainable career in the industry.

About the Illustrator

Matthew Salaiz is a veterinary practice manager who has been an active member of the veterinary field since he was fourteen years old. He is passionate about making an impact in the veterinary field through community service, by facilitating, coordinating, and participating in various activities.

Salaiz "fills his balloons" with art and music, as well as with outdoor activities such as hiking, camping, and fishing. His biggest "balloon-filler," however, is the love for his soul dog Pancho, who posed as the loose model for the illustrations in "The Unspoken Life", the first publication for the 1 Life Connected movement. California native, Salaiz lives in the Central Valley.

Are you ready to cross the bridge back to connection?

1 Life Connected offers resources to help you on your journey, including:

◊ *"The Unspoken Life" - a resource available through amazon. com, which allows you to begin the journey towards connection*

◊ *Free worksheets and support for you to navigate the message on your own*

◊ *A member-supported community of connected veterinary professionals on Facebook*

◊ *Videos, forums, and other resources for individual veterinary professionals and teams*

◊ *Balloon challenges such as the "Take a Bubble Break", to get you and your team started on balloon filling activities*

◊ *Customized support to bring you and your team back to connection*

You can also connect with Dr. Kimberly Pope-Robinson through:

◊ *In-person speaking engagements for your organization*

◊ *Life coaching to recognize, embrace, and overcome challenges*

◊ *Retreats with like-minded veterinarians on the path back to connection*

To learn more, visit www.1Lifecc.Com or email Dr. Pope at k.pope-robinson@1lifecc.com